A Brighter Tomorrow

If you're reading this book, it means you've experienced or witnessed a tragic event. You might be scared, shocked, angry, or not know how you feel. Allow the activities in this book to guide you through your fears and help you begin the healing process.

A Tragic Event

Sometimes, the feelings we're left with after something bad happens are so strong we can't think or feel anything else. Your feelings are your feelings, and they're not wrong.

I am mostly feeling _____ .

In the box below, draw a picture of how you're feeling TODAY.

Are you having a hard time talking about the event? Start by drawing something you remember from the tragic event. It can be anything.

Do you have trouble sleeping at night? Is it hard to fall asleep, or do you have bad dreams that wake you up?

Draw what you think about when you're trying to go to sleep at night.

Draw or write what happens in one of your bad dreams.

Just the Facts!

Sometimes, sticking with the facts is easier than talking about how the event makes you feel. Fill out the cloud shapes below with answers about the event you experienced. If you get stuck, ask someone you trust for help.

Who?

What?

Where?

When?

Why?

Here's more room to journal about the facts of the event:

_____

_____

_____

_____

_____

_____

_____

_____

_____

_____

_____

_____

_____

All the facts in the world can't tell you how to feel, but writing them down can begin to make you feel better. Do you feel differently now that you've written down what happened? Draw how you're feeling now.

Sort It Out

How did such a tragic event happen? Can you explain it? This is the place to write down your questions and your fears.

_____

_____

_____

_____

_____

Often, we get stuck on 'why' because we want there to be a reason. We want to be able to work it out in our heads. Do you have an idea about why the tragic event happened?

_____

_____

_____

_____

_____

Turn Back the Clock

Turn back the clock.

Don't let it stop,

Until time is back

To the day before it all went away.

I can start over

My world will be right,

Nothing will be wrong

The hurt will be gone.

My friends will be here.

We'll be having such fun.

There will be no sideways glances,

Or people who keep asking if I'm okay.

Turn back the clock

I just want it all to go away.

How does this poem make you feel? Do you agree or disagree with it?

Feelings can be scary to think or talk about. Learning about your feelings and why you have them can help you feel better.

Circle any of the STRONG feelings you're having now. Write any other strong feelings that aren't listed around the lightning bolt.

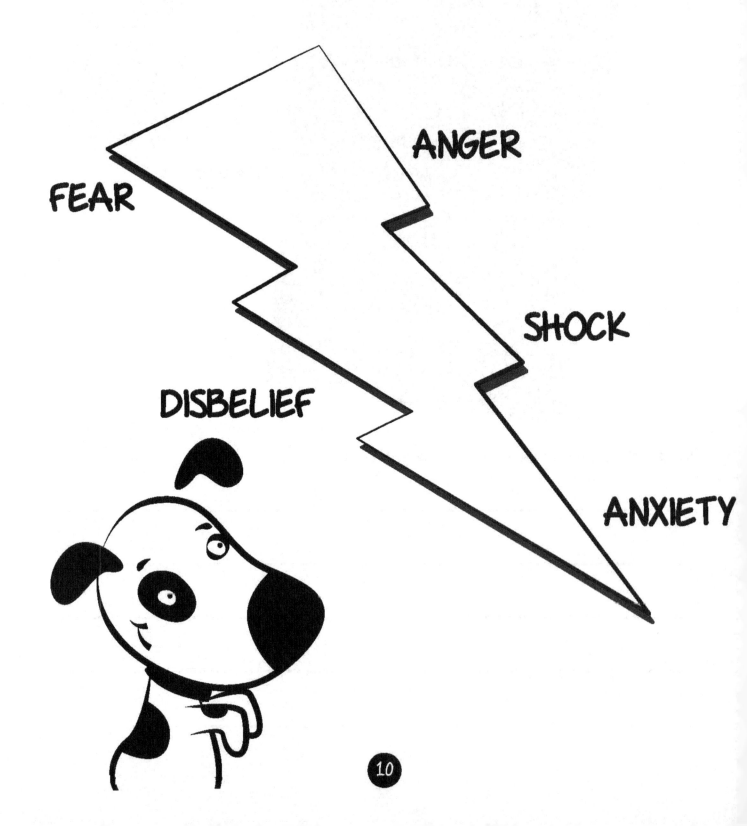

ANGER

FEAR

SHOCK

DISBELIEF

ANXIETY

There are other feelings and emotions you may have right now. Circle the other feelings you're having now. Write some other feelings in the blanks, as well.

nervous   sad   lonely   lost

guilty   torn   helpless

afraid   _____

_____   _____

Which feelings from this page and the previous page are you having the hardest time accepting? Write them below, and then talk about them with someone you trust.

_____

_____

_____

_____

_____

Pretend someone took your picture at each time period described below. How have you changed? Write about how you felt in each box.

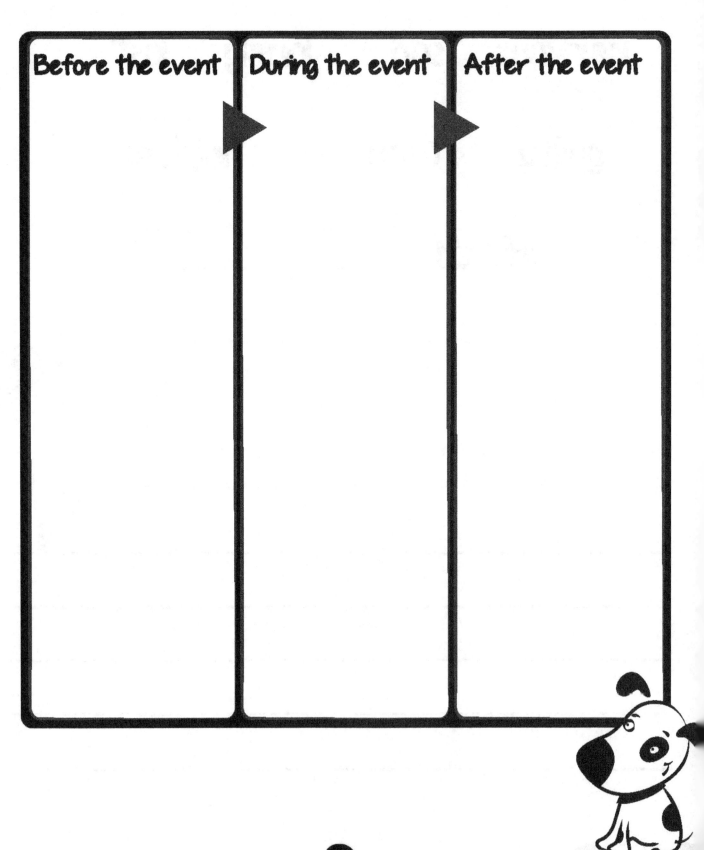

Before the event	During the event	After the event

Since the traumatic event, how have you changed?

Are you STRONGER or WEAKER? How?

_____

_____

_____

Are you more or less PATIENT? How?

_____

_____

_____

Are you more TRUSTING or more SUSPICOUS? How?

_____

_____

_____

Have there been any other changes?

_____

_____

_____

You may think the life you had before the tragic event is gone forever. Write or draw the differences in your life in the chart below.

Life Before	Life After

Looking at the chart on the previous page, is there anything about your old self that you miss?

_____

_____

_____

_____

_____

Is there something you admire about the new you?

_____

_____

_____

_____

If the You of Today, who'd just experienced something terrible, could write a letter to the You of the Past, what would you say?

Dear Me,

_____

_____

_____

_____

_____

_____

_____

_____

_____

_____

Love,

_____

Do you feel like everyone is talking to you differently now? Most are only trying to help — they just may not know how. Can you help them? Write what they say to you in the speech bubbles on the left, and then write what you wish they'd say in the thought bubbles on the right.

Often, the worst part of being a witness to or part of a traumatic event is the feeling of helplessness. Maybe you wish you could've done something to help, even though you really couldn't. What do you feel the most helpless about? Write or draw your answers below.

Do you replay what happened in your mind, trying to find a better ending? Pretend you're writing a script for a movie below. What different ending would you make if you could?

_____

_____

_____

_____

_____

_____

_____

_____

_____

_____

_____

_____

_____

Can you think of a movie or book where a character either witnessed or experienced a traumatic event?

What was the movie and character, what happened, and how did the character react?

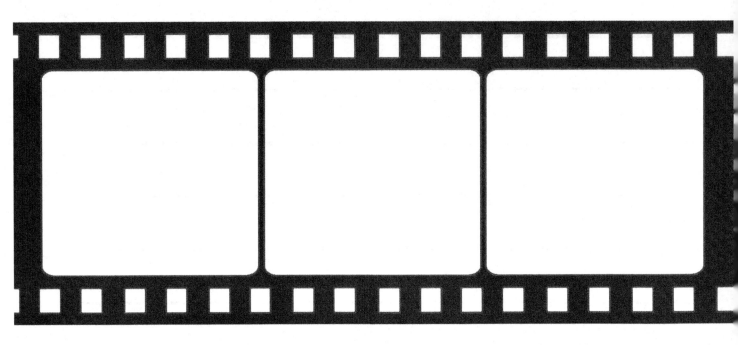

Can you learn anything from that character's experiences and apply it to where you are right now?

_____

_____

_____

_____

_____

_____

When something terrible happens, we oftentimes feel powerless. Draw yourself as a Superhero! Someone who is strong and powerful.

If you had ONE wish that could be granted right now, what would you wish for?
Draw or write your wish in the star below.

Who or what do you miss the most right now?
Draw and write about it below.

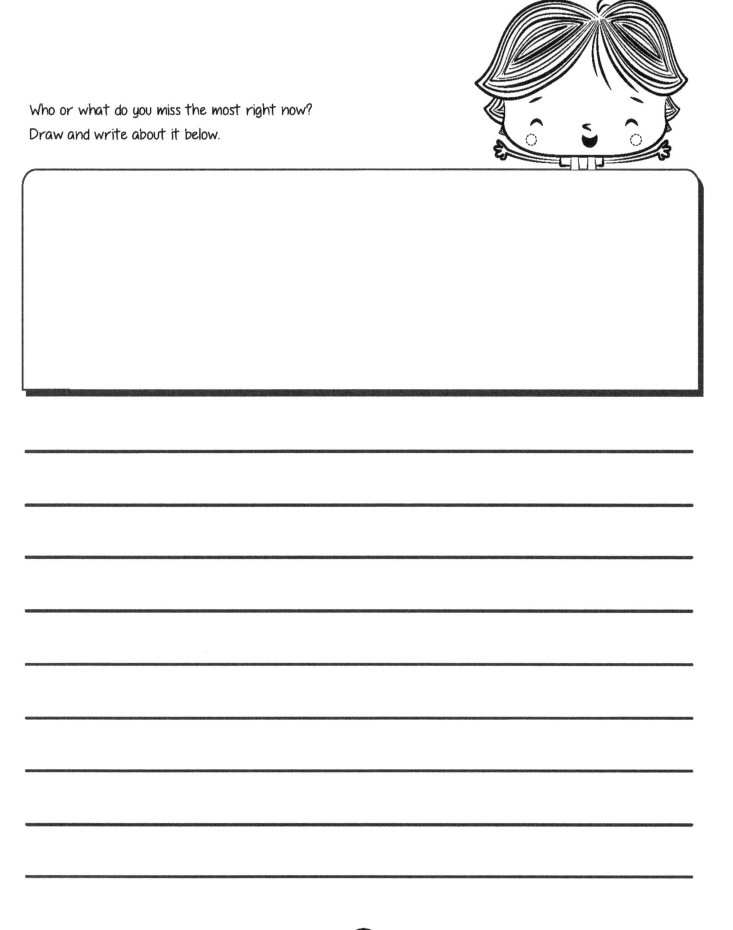

Do you feel broken, like parts of you aren't the same anymore since the tragedy? Maybe you feel you're not as trusting or hopeful. Finish drawing the circle below, then write or draw what you think would make you feel whole inside.

Sometimes we all need a HUG, especially when we're confused, worried, or afraid. Draw a picture of someone you love and trust giving you a big bear hug.

In the following boxes, write down someone at each location who makes you feel safe and secure.

Home

School

In the Car

Grandparent's House

It's important to know that traumatic events happen unexpectedly. Work with your family to create a safety plan. Write down your thoughts and ideas below, and then share them with your loved ones.

- _____
- _____
- _____
- _____
- _____
- _____
- _____
- _____
- _____
- _____

After thinking about how you can help yourself, can you begin to see how strong you are? Write down a few of your strengths in the circles below. As you go through your journey, you may find even more. When this happens, just add more circles!

Draw a picture of something that makes you SMILE.

Get Active and Stay Busy

Find activities you enjoy doing and activities that make you feel better: reading, dancing, exercising, and talking with friends. It's good to stay busy after something terrible happens. You don't want to spend all your energy and attention on the traumatic experience. Make a list of things you enjoy doing. Try to do at least three of these every week.

1. _____

2. _____

3. _____

4. _____

5. _____

6. _____

7. _____

8. _____

Talk It Out

Having family and trust adults around is very important. Whom can you go to for a talk or to feel safe? Write the names of people you trust in the hearts below. These people are your support team.

Below are words that might remind you of feeling safe. Circle the words that remind you of safety. Color in the words you feel when you're in your safe place with safe people.

warm   comforted

sheltered   satisfied

secure   protected

shielded   free

You can find friends at school, in your neighborhood, at sports activities, or at other clubs. Having friends you can laugh with, joke with, and have fun with can really help to lighten your mood.

Do you have friends you can be yourself with? Write the names of three of your friends in the arrows below, and write two facts about each of them next to the dots.

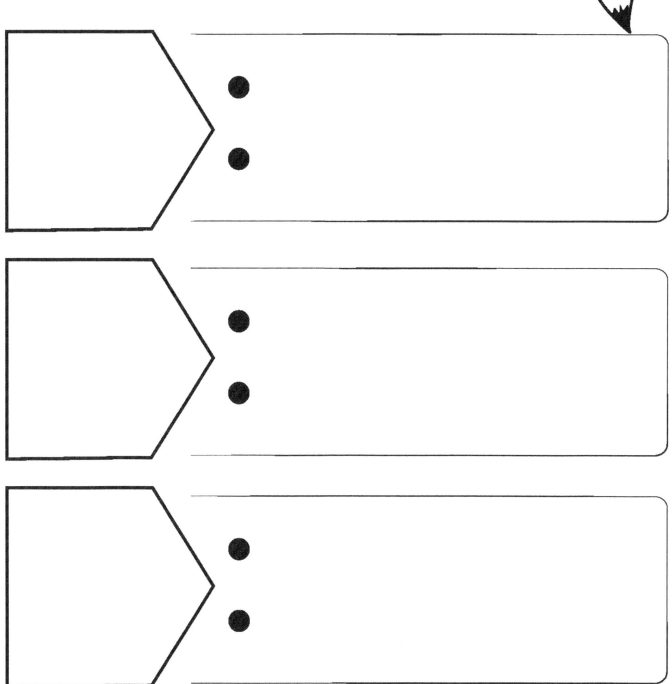

Write a letter of thanks to someone who helped during the tragedy.

Dear _____,

_____

_____

_____

_____

_____

_____

_____

_____

_____

_____

_____

Thank you,

_____

Pretend you can say anything you want to two people you love and trust. They never have to see this, unless you want to show them. What would you say? Write your answers below.

To _____

To _____

Draw pictures of fun times you've had with the people with whom you feel safest. Know that no matter what, you have a support team.

Good Times!

Even though many activities in this workbook remind you of a time you may rather not think about, working through the events and feelings helps you heal and move forward. Now, you have a completed workbook that you can look back on every time you need to remember how far you've come!

REMEMBER: Be STRONG because tomorrow will be a brighter day!

A Brighter Tomorrow: A Workbook to Help Kids Cope with Traumatic Events

ISBN-10: 061598357X

BISAC: Juvenile Nonfiction / Health & Daily Living / General

Printed in the United States of America

CPSIA information can be obtained at www.ICGtesting.com
Printed in the USA
LVOW03s1517220915

455243LV00016B/494/P